To: Sister
Angel Mason

From: Sister Joy

I will always love
Thanks 4 your Support

God Taught Me: He's My Provider

by Regina Hughes

Copyright © 2008 by Regina Hughes

ISBN 0-7414-4396-1

Published by:

PUBLISHING.COM

1094 New DeHaven Street, Suite 100
West Conshohocken, PA 19428-2713
Info@buybooksontheweb.com
www.buybooksontheweb.com
Toll-free (877) BUY BOOK
Local Phone (610) 941-9999
Fax (610) 941-9959

Printed in the United States of America

Printed on Recycled Paper

Published July 2008

TABLE OF CONTENTS

THANK YOU

Thanks and appreciation to Almighty God, the giver of gifts and talents. I acknowledge that God has truly been my provider. To my wonderful, supportive husband Elder Powell J. Hughes for much encouragement and who has been my friend through this time, my children Shanika and Jermiane Hughes, who without there different decisions in life would not have inspired me to write this book.

IN LOVING MEMORY

This book is dedicated to my natural mother Dorothy Jean Alexander who went through much sickness with cancer, but she always depended on God to be her provider of wealth, strength, faith and courage; showing me how to depend on almighty God as my provider. Whenever I had to preach or commentate, she was there with her beautiful smile to brighten up my day. She is with Almighty God no longer here with me in the natural. But, I will always have my memories. She knew I was writing this book and gave me support. Thank you mom for not giving up on the gift that God has given to me. To God be the glory.

THANK YOU

Thank you to my loving pastor's Donald Coleman, Sr., and in Memory of Co-Pastor April Coleman who has gone on to be with the Lord, she was a tower of strength while she was here and my Bara Church family. Thank you to my precious friend and confidant Elder Gail Williams, who is also my trusted editor. She always had faith in what God has given me and appreciates the call of God on my life. Also, a special thanks to my Spiritual mother Elder Lauren Triplett for much love, wisdom, correction and guidance. She always keeps me balanced. She is the prayer warrior in my families' life, a mother to me, at all times.

FOREWORD

We all know that God has chosen us before we were even born. I am thrilled and excited to know that you have allowed the Lord to use you in such a way as this. This book is enjoyable and full of quality information. "God Taught Me, He's My Provider", is written to simplify the wise. As you turn the pages you will realize that God has allowed some uncomplicated revelation and truth to be revealed, and at the same time making sure that you do not ignore the voice of God. As you read through this book realize and remember to not be slothful in business; but be fervent in spirit; serving the Lord.

Elder Gail Williams
Detroit, MI
November, 2005

INTRODUCTION

How it all began. I'm in my prayer time July 31, 2001 9:00a.m. The voice of my Holy Father speaks. It's time to write. I asked the Lord is this message for me or for someone else in your body. He reply's no my child it is for you. This is how it began.

Two years ago in the month of June I decided I wanted a higher paying job, because my husband and I just purchased a new home and car, without praying I began my journey (to look for another job). I didn't have to look far; I found a position very quickly and was hired. I was on a two week vacation before I was to start my new job. The first day of my vacation 9:00a.m. prayer time I'm weeping in the presence of the Lord. A voice comes and speaks to me and says, that job you are about to take is not yours. At that time I could not discern if that was the voice of the Lord, I replied Satan get out of my prayer time with God, and you are not welcome here. The thought of me not being able to work was not something I was comfortable with. So, all that day I kept saying could that be you God? Then I would reply no way Father you would never tell me not to take my new job. You just blessed us with a new home, a new car and if I'm not working we will not be able to pay our mortgage, car payment, or other bills.

So, Tuesday Morning 9:00a.m., I start my prayer time all over again. The weeping started again in the presence of the Lord, and once again I hear this voice. Immediately, I began to stop weeping and I prayed Heavenly Father, in the name of Jesus is this you talking to me, pleased give me your word. He gave me *I Samuel 15:22* *"Behold to obey is better than sacrifice."* So, this time I knew that it was my Lord and I obeyed. I called a very dear prayer partner to pray with me, I told her what the Lord has asked me to do, she already knew about it. The Lord had her praying for me to come into agreement with what He wanted me to do concerning his perfect will.

The war began in my members the flesh and the Spirit. Outwardly, I did not have a job but inside my mind I was going crazy with who's going to pay these bills. I did not know how to trust God this way. I was leaning to my own understanding I was not acknowledging God so that he could direct my path. By January 2000 I began to think that I could go back to work. This trusting in God was not something that I wanted to do, because I did not understand what God was trying to teach me. I called my employer back and she gave me a job. But little did I know what was going to happen next. Once again I'm in my prayer time and I began to weep because I knew that I was out of the will of God. Every night when I began to sleep I could not rest. I was being tormented by evil spirits, because I had iniquity in my heart (self will) I began to pray with an open heart and mind father help me to understand your will for my life at this time. True repentance always moves the heart of God. Then the Lord began to show me in his word about faith, trust, love, endurance and Godly sorrow and how that He was my provider. Through the pages you are about to read hearken your heart to here the word of the Lord.

CHAPTER 1

HEARING AND SUBMITTING TO THE VOICE OF THE FATHER

The first thing that we are going to talk about is discernment. When the voice of the Lord comes to you will you be like young Samuel? Samuel did not know the voice of God, because he was not mature in the things of God and *(did not have a personal relationship with Him)*. In order to know the voice of God you must know the word and you must know his character. In order to know the voice of God you must be taught; to be taught you must have a teacher. That will only come by spending quality time with the Father in prayer and in studying the word of God. Often times I tell my children, if you love someone you will want to spend as much time with them as you can.

1 Samuel (3:1-5)

And the child Samuel ministered to the LORD before Eli. And the word of the LORD was rare in those days; there was no widespread revelation. And it came to pass at that time, while Eli was lying down in his place, and when his eyes had begun to grow so dim that he could not see, and before the lamp of God went out in the tabernacle of the LORD where the ark of God was, and while Samuel was lying down, that the LORD called Samuel. And he answered, "Here I am!" So he ran to Eli and said, "Here I am, for you called me." And he said, "I did not call; lie down again." And he went and lay down.

Discernment

The word discernment means the act of discerning the power or faculty of the mind by which it distinguishes one thing from another; Capable of seeing in the Spirit; knowing and judging: sharp – sighted and the power to perceive.

So many times in our Christian walk with the Lord we want the power, but we do not want to have a personal relationship with God. We only want to do what feels comfortable to us. Well take it from this woman of God; you must come out of your comfort zone. If you do not have discernment you will be tossed to and fro by every wind of doctrine. You will run from church to church because you will not have a developed mind in the things of God to know that you are not to go any where or do any thing without seeking the face of our Heavenly Father first. Also, you must be under the correct shepherd to help you learn how to hear from the Lord. When young Samuel could not discern the voice of the Lord he went to his teacher the Priest Eli *(this was the only voice he was used to hearing)*.

You must be conditioned to hearing God's voice.

Before you will be able to submit, you must learn to be a servant.

And the LORD came, and stood, and called as at other times, Samuel, Samuel. Then Samuel answered, Speak; for thy servant heareth. (1 Samuel 3:10)

This passage of scripture is the key to many of the people of God's breakthrough. Before Samuel could learn to submit to God, he had to learn to submit to an earthly teacher. Samuel learned to be available to Eli; he is now immediately available to the Lord. Samuel learned servant hood and submission. Saints of God you must learn to submit to the leader's that God has put in your life *(your Pastor's # 1)*.

How can you expect God to bless your life or elevate you to your next level when you have not conquered your self? Yes your own will. It is not about what you think; it is about what God requires for you to do.

Example of waiting until your turn:

Now after the death of Moses the servant of the LORD, it came to pass that the LORD spoke to Joshua the son of Nun, Moses' minister, saying: *"Moses My servant is dead. Now therefore, arise, go over this Jordan, you and all this people, to the land which I am giving to them-- the children of Israel. (Joshua 1:1-2)*

Joshua is a very excellent example of patience. Joshua served 40 years under the leadership of Moses. We as saints today don't even want to wait a day. Remember also that before Moses died he laid hands on Joshua.

And Joshua the son of Nun was full of the spirit of wisdom; for Moses had laid his hands upon him: and the children of Israel hearkened unto him, and did as the LORD commanded Moses. (Deuteronomy 34:9)

It's very important to note that you pray for God to put you under a pastor that He has for you. Because your pastor is the one that God is going to use to help you find your destiny. Without Moses, Joshua would have never gotten the impartation that God had for him, remember it's your pastor. Pray and seek the face of God like never before, put your will down. The pastor is the vessel that God is going to use.

The word of God also teaches us not to be anxious for nothing, but in everything by prayer and supplication with thanksgiving, let your request be made known unto God. Go to your Heavenly Father, and it shall be given you. Seek and ye shall find; knock and it shall be opened unto you. Remember when you go to our Heavenly Father; go with a pure heart, and right motives.

Who shall ascend into the hill of the LORD? or who shall stand in his holy place? He that hath clean hands, and a pure heart; who hath not lifted up his soul unto vanity, nor sworn deceitfully. (Psalms 24:3-4)

You must understand that everyone can not go into the presence of the Most High God. Those who can enter into the presence of God are those who have conducted their daily life with integrity. Joshua and Samuel's life were great examples of integrity. The reason I know this is because the word of God tells us that they learned how to hear the voice of the Lord through someone else that God used in their lives. They were servants first, and that's how it has to begin. In order for you to hear God's voice and submit to it you must be a servant and have a teachable spirit.

PRINCIPLES FOR CHAPTER 1

1. Samuel was a child.

2. He went to the voice in which he was familiar with.

3. He needed an earthly teacher.

4. Eli had to perceive for him, until he learned in the things of God.

5. He was told to answer as a servant.

CHAPTER 2

LEARNING TO STUDY AND PRAY THE WORD OF GOD

II Timothy 2:15

Study to shew thyself approved unto God, a workman that needeth not to be ashamed, rightly dividing the word of truth.

A lot of our problems we have when we pray come from wrong study habits.

How can you expect to get answers to prayer when you don't even have our Heavenly Father's precious word down in your spirit?

You must learn the importance of taking out time to get in the word so that you will have the mind of God when you come before the Father with your request.

Study

The act in which you use your mind to acquire knowledge, you must also understand what you are reading in the word of God, be patient. Read the word over and over until you have peace in your mind and spirit about the passage you are studying. Also, before you even begin to study ask God to give you the spirit of wisdom, knowledge and understanding. That way God along with the Holy Spirit can help you as you study the word of God.

The word of God, is the only conclusive source of wisdom, knowledge and understanding concerning ultimate realities.

You must understand our Heavenly Father wants you to fulfill your purpose in life. But! He will not force you to read his word; it has to be a desire that you must have. I would have never gotten to know my wonderful Heavenly Father as my provider if I would have not first learned to study. So when I pray I believe that I receive what ever I ask according to his will because HE taught me how to study. Now I know how to pray. See the Holy Spirit illuminated my small thinking, so whatever my father tells me to pray for, I study the scriptures concerning that matter and I waited for God to bring forth the manifestation of that prayer that I am praying. How can I know what belongs to me if I don't read my bible to find what the father has promise me.

> **Not slothful in business; fervent in spirit; serving the Lord**
> **Rom 12:11**

This passage simply means don't be lazy when it comes to the things of God.

Take it from this woman of God, my Heavenly Father taught me in order to pray the heart of God you must have the mind of God. In order to have the mind of God, you must have the Spirit of God. In order to have the Spirit of God you must have the Word of God. I pray the word of God because of training through the school of the Holy Spirit and being under some very anointed men and women of God. You must understand how important it is for yourself, not to be boastful or arrogant it's for growth and development.

I have also found out that when you spend time learning the word of God you find so much help for daily living. I learned in my time of testing, God desires the best for his children. What father do you know who loves his children will not provide for them. But don't be ignorant you must be an obedient child, yes even in kingdom living there are rules. What God has for you is for you. Don't focus on someone else's blessing. Seek him and find out what he has for you. Don't feel stupid when you don't understand something in your bible. The disciples asked Jesus to teach them to pray.

Luke 11:1

And it came to pass, that, as he was praying in a certain place, when he ceased, one of his disciples said unto him, Lord, teach us to pray, as John also taught his disciples.

Now that you see he had to teach his disciples, that let's you know that you must also be taught. Now if you need prayer because you are having problems understanding God's word let us pray.

Father in the name of your son Jesus teach us to pray your will, give us divine understanding of what we should be praying for in our lives and in the lives of your people. Amen.

Note!

Praise and Worship should always be a part of your study time with the Lord.

Since God is enthroned in our praises, worship is the key to entering fully into his presence; I have found that out when I needed a breakthrough from God in areas where I am barren. Worship has always been the key to get the attention of my father. When you dare to worship our Heavenly Father in the face of pain and suffering you let God know that you have not lost hope. See, you must understand what worship releases; is the glory of God, thus bringing the worshipers, actualized responses of his kingly reign. Sing in your time of barrenness.

8

Isaiah 54:1

Sing, O barren, thou that didst not bear; break forth into singing, and cry aloud, thou that didst not travail with child: for more are the children of the desolate than the children of the married wife, saith the LORD.

Barren – unproductive, unfruitful, unprofitable, empty.

To deal with barrenness use worship. Remember worship ushers you into the presence of the Lord and what ever you need from the Lord; He is willing to give you when it is true worship. Worship releases his miraculous provision, you may need peace, you may need joy, and whatever you need God has it.

Isaiah 54:10

[10]For the mountains shall depart, and the hills be removed; but my kindness shall not depart from thee, neither shall the covenant of my peace be removed, saith the LORD that hath mercy on thee.

It is the desire of our Lord that you will live a life of peace. Here we see that our Lord is giving restoration to Jerusalem. Don't you know he wants to restore his children back to himself? Remember you must be in right standing with God. If you want to obtain mercy you must repent for not walking in love with your brother, sister, husband, wife and children; the way that our Heavenly Father has called us to walk in. You must learn to forgive not with your mouth but with your heart.

PRINCIPLES FOR CHAPTER 2

1. When you study you will not have to be ashamed, no guilt, and no condemnation will be present.

2. Do not be slothful concerning the things of God.

3. Worship should always be a part of your study time.

4. In times of barrenness, worship God.

CHAPTER 3

CONFIDENCE EQUAL POWER WHEN YOU PRAY THE WORD OF GOD

So many times when believers pray they don't pray with confidence. Now, I want you to search your heart. Do you really believe when you pray the word of God that it is going to happen? No or Yes.

Well, I am going to help you!

When you pray with confidence it means you are trusting in God to bring your prayer to past. Saints our God knows everything you have need of before you ask.

Matt 6:32

32(For after all these things do the Gentiles seek :) for your heavenly Father knoweth that ye have need of all these things.

Hebrews 10:35-37

35 Cast not away therefore your confidence, which hath great recompense of reward. 36For ye have need of patience, that, after ye have done the will of God, ye might receive the promise. 37For yet a little while, and he that shall come will come, and will not tarry.

Verse 35 tells us not to cast away our confidence. It's simple! Don't stop trusting in God's word. No matter what the enemy tries to put in your mind, because if you don't give up, look at what is waiting for you, (great recompense) of reward.

Sometimes we have to lose something, in order to gain greater in God. I know it can get hard, when you're doing the will of God. That's one reason why the Lord put on my heart to write this book. Don't think that I have arrived because I have not. But the one thing I learned in all of my hardships is to don't stop having confidence in my prayers, I know my father hears me when I pray. I may not get what I am asking for at that time, but I know its coming, because, I'm praying his will and that's enough to bring peace to my day. If it doesn't come today I pray again the next day, until God brings his word to past.

Verse 36 says for ye have need of patience. A lot of times God can not give us what we ask for at that time, because we are not ready. Understand your Father's purpose; He wants to allow the fruit of the spirit to work in your life, and patience is one of them. I was never a patient person, what ever I wanted, I wanted it yesterday. How many of you know that's not the will of God? We make major mistakes in our lives because we are not willing to wait. Please saints of God, Stop! Doing everything in your life without consulting your Father.

If you are going to gain the greater good, you must learn to pray with confidence. Take that step today trust in God. The power of a saint praying with confidence is the will of the father. What father do you know that does not want his child to have confidence; and watch what God release to you?

Verse 37 *For yet a little while, and he that shall come, will come and will not tarry.* You realize that it's in the little while where God has done the most work in you. You might think he's delaying, but he is not.

[6]But without faith it is impossible to please him: for he that cometh to God must believe that he is, and that he is a rewarder of them that diligently seek him. Hebrew 11:6

Rewarder of them that <u>diligently</u> <u>seek</u> <u>him</u>

Diligent

Steady in application to be attentive, done with care and constant effort.

Greek term: Ek-zeteo – investigate, crave, to search out, demand. Seek after carefully.

There will always be a reward from our father when you choose to seek him. But you must understand it must be with your whole heart, your motive must be pure. Don't seek after him for things, seek after your father because you love him and you want a relationship with him. The word of God teaches that God knows your inward thoughts. I know not what I should pray for, but the Holy Spirit teaches me how I should pray.

Now it's time to go to the throne of grace that we may obtain mercy from our heavenly father. Use me for your glory; allow me to be a vessel that has been tried by fire. It's my desire to come with pure motives before you father. You are Holy and I too must be Holy to come in your presence.

PRINCIPLES FOR CHAPTER 3

1. When God tells you he's going to do something, don't give up, and hold on to the promises of God.

2. You must have the fruit of patience when you stand on the promises of God.

3. You must have **FAITH**.

4. You must be diligent about the things of God.

CHAPTER 4

SAY NO TO YOUR FLESH

As I am writing I pray that our precious Lord and Savior Jesus Christ would help you from giving into your flesh. Remember the final decision is yours.

I John 2:15-17

¹⁵Love not the world, neither the things that are in the world. If any man love the world, the love of the Father is not in him.

¹⁶For all that is in the world, the lust of the flesh, and the lust of the eyes, and the pride of life, is not of the Father, but is of the world.

¹⁷And the world passeth away, and the lust thereof: but he that doeth the will of God abideth for ever.

So many times in our lives as Christians we allow too many earthly things to get in the way of what God wants to do in our lives.

In I John 2:16 it talks about what is in the world and not to lust after them. Let's talk about it. Do you understand what it means to lust after something? It means the following:

1. To have an intense desire

2. Over mastering desire

3. Lust also mean's eagerness to possess or enjoy

In other words you want to do what you want to do. More than you want to do what God wants you to do. That's why the flesh is an enemy to God; you must put it under subjection.

The bible tells us also in Matthews 6:33 seek ye first the kingdom of God, and his righteousness; and all these things shall be added unto you. You see saints when you seek after something it's a desire that you have. I am not going to complicate the word of God because our father did not do it. Turn your desires away from things of the world and seek after righteousness, then you will have joy, then you will have peace because that's what God desires for his children to have. God desires relationship with you, ask the Holy Spirit to lead you into the truth, don't allow your flesh to keep you from the perfect will of our Father.

So many times in our lives as saints of the Most High God, we allow these three things to get in the way:

1. The lust of flesh

2. The lust of the eyes

3. The pride of life

The thing that God wants us to understand is he has already given us power over our flesh. It is up to us to yield to the Spirit. You see, the war has already been won for you, now let's look at what God says in Roman 8:5; 8:11.

Roman 8:5; 8:11.

⁵For they that are after the flesh do mind the things of the flesh; but they that are after the Spirit the things of the Spirit.

¹¹But if the Spirit of him that raised up Jesus from the dead dwell in you, he that raised up Christ from the dead shall also quicken your mortal bodies by his Spirit that dwelleth in you

Roman 8:11 but if the Spirit of him that raised up Jesus from the dead dwell in you, listen to this point.

Do you understand the spirit the word is talking about, the spirit of the Most High God, Jehovah Jereh? He provided life to Jesus what makes you think that he will not do the same for you. Remember! There is all power given to God. The earth is the Lords and the fullness thereof; the world and they that dwell there in, come on saints of God just have faith in God it's not hard. Just learn to speak the word and apply it to your life daily. I know for a fact you are going to come through because Jehovah Jereh is with you.

The best example that the bible gives in saying no to the flesh was our Lord and Savior Jesus. Let's go to the garden.

Mark 14:34-36

^{34}And saith unto them, My soul is exceeding sorrowful unto death: tarry ye here, and watch.

^{35}And he went forward a little, and fell on the ground, and prayed that, if it were possible, the hour might pass from him.

^{36}And he said, Abba, Father, all things are possible unto thee; take away this cup from me: nevertheless not what I will, but what thou wilt.

Don't think for one moment that our Lord and Savior can't be touched by what you are going through.

Hebrew 4:15

^{15}For we have not an high priest which cannot be touched with the feeling of our infirmities; but was in all points tempted like as we are, yet without sin.

Let me give you more information about the flesh. In order to put your flesh under subjection you must understand the characteristics of your flesh:

Galatians 5:19-21

[19]Now the works of the flesh are manifest, which are these; Adultery, fornication, uncleanness, lasciviousness, [20]Idolatry, witchcraft, hatred, variance, emulations, wrath, strife, seditions, heresies, [21]Envyings, murders, drunkenness, revellings, and such like: of the which I tell you before, as I have also told you in time past, that they which do such things shall not inherit the kingdom of God.

The reason I listed each of the root works of the flesh, so if God wants to deal with you on one of them as you read, study what God is saying to you, ask God to give you understanding and turn from the works of the flesh. So! You can begin a closer walk with our Heavenly Father.

So many times as I have been studying the word of God the Holy Spirit would say that's you and I begin to repent, and ask God to set me free. Just say yes to God, and say no to your flesh. It's not as hard to say when you know about the many blessings that are waiting for you on other side of the mountain.

The main reason why you will not say yes to our Heavenly Father's will is because you keep giving into the desire of your flesh. That's where you place your trust.

That is right; you trust in your flesh, but now its time for you to pray to the father about why you put your trust in your flesh.

Come on go before your Father and have a talk with him. Its time for that talk, He has what you need just ask him.

PRINCIPLES FOR CHAPTER 4

1. You must learn to crucify your flesh daily.

2. Seek Righteousness.

3. Jesus in the Garden of Gethsemane is your example of how to let your will die.

CHAPTER 5

COMING INTO THE LIGHT

Act 26:13-18

13At midday, O king, I saw in the way a light from heaven, above the brightness of the sun, shining round about me and them which journeyed with me. 14And when we were all fallen to the earth, I heard a voice speaking unto me, and saying in the Hebrew tongue, Saul, Saul, why persecutest thou me? it is hard for thee to kick against the pricks.

15And I said, Who art thou, Lord? And he said, I am Jesus whom thou persecutest. 16But rise, and stand upon thy feet: for I have appeared unto thee for this purpose, to make thee a minister and a witness both of these things which thou hast seen, and of those things in the which I will appear unto thee;

17Delivering thee from the people, and from the Gentiles, unto whom now I send thee, 18To open their eyes, and to turn them from darkness to light, and from the power of Satan unto God, that they may receive forgiveness of sins, and inheritance among them which are sanctified by faith that is in me.

When I look at verse's 13-18 these are some thoughts that come into my spirit. When you come into the light others will also see the light around you. The light is also always, undeniable; it represents the Glory of God. The power brought Paul and his companions off their horses and to their knees reverence and display of God's awesome impact. It was when the light came that Paul discerned the voice of a higher power was speaking to him. His question who art thou Lord, let's us know that. Revelation comes whenever the light is present.

It's God trying to get your attention. In Paul's case God came to reveal his purpose for Paul's life. His destiny was to be a witness and a minister. Instruction also came with the light. And most of all the light comes to transform from darkness.

Coming into the light will always cause you to give up your past.

I can remember the day of my own conversion from the darkness. It was the most beautiful experience I ever had. I was living a life of sin. I was not happy; I was full of bitterness from past relationships. Thank God for intercessors, because my best friend had gotten saved and was praying for me. Then she asked me to go to church with her, and I went. It was strange to me because I was used to one way of church then I walked into the sanctuary and much to my surprise there was only ten people inside. When the preacher began to preach my heart was touched and when they had alter call the Spirit led me up there. The Pastor prayed over me and I fell out. Something so wonderful was going on in my Spirit, I was being changed from darkness and God was showing me the light. I have been walking with the Lord every since. Yes, like Paul I have many things that I must suffer for the sake of Jesus Christ. See, saints of god so many times we think that we have arrived, but take it from this woman of faith, the way up, is down on your knees. Stay in the presence of the Lord every chance you get, that is the only way that you stay humble. When Paul heard the voice of Jesus he could not refuse the Master's voice. He trembled, Jesus told him about his self; he exposed him in front of the others that he was with. I found out saints, like Paul it is had to kick against the pricks – or goads. A goad is a pointed stick for urging on a team of oxen. This may mean that Paul was already having his conscience pricked about the terrible things he was doing.

I also remember telling the Pastor that I was under at that time that I needed more of God. I started to realize that something was missing in my Christian walk I was seeking to be filled with the Spirit of the living God. There was such loneliness at that time in my life. I did not understand spiritually or what it was.

I thank God that he saw my longing for the light. There must be a conversion from darkness. There is so much that our father desires for his children. We must learn to let go, to let God shape us into that beautiful person that he desires us to be.

Come into the light don't go half way, let's walk all the way in. Trust our Father to take care of you. The most important thing we can do is be the light on the earth that our Father in heaven has called us to be. He called us to be children of light to a dying world in need of a Savior. Let God use you for his glory, that's your purpose to be a help to this dying world. Our Father in heaven can use you any way that He desires, you may not be able to preach like Paul, but you may have a smile that he wants to develop, that can help people find their way to God. So many times the father has used people to smile and say hi and people say hi back, tell you their name, next thing you know you are telling them about Jesus. Jesus is the reason you have that smile. They told you all their problems just because you are anointed with a smile. God has so many ways' to use his vessels; you don't have to be in a pulpit to do the work of the Lord. So ask the Father to take the blinders off your eyes and show you the light (*your true purpose*).

Matthew 5:14

Ye are the light of the world……..

Because you are that child of light that God Has called you to be!

PRINCIPLES FOR CHAPTER 5

1. When light first comes to darkness it can be blinding.

2. The Light will always expose you to the truth.

3. When the light comes get ready for commitment.

CHAPTER 6

THE WILDERNESS

No Operation – No Manifestation

On the wonderful journey with God, there is going to be a wilderness test:

Matt 4:1

Then was Jesus led up of the Spirit into the wilderness to be tempted of the devil.

Example #1 Jesus

Jesus is our perfect example that you can not escape your time of wilderness testing. If you are going to be used as a vessel, the test will surely come. Remember in order to go from glory to glory you must be broken. The wilderness prepares you for what's a head of you. Take the example of the olive, when they are processing them for oil they crush them. Now, look at your own life, your will must be crushed, that's why you need the wilderness test. Also the oil represents the anointing. The word of God teaching us the anointing is what destroys yoke. You can not have true ministry without the power of God present.

The wilderness is where the operation will take place. Remember our Lord and Savior was lead by the Spirit into the wilderness as an example to us. That's why it is vital for you to get your heart and mind lined up with the word of God. When Jesus came out of the wilderness what did he use against the enemy? The word of God.

Matt 4:3-4

3   The tempter came to him, he said, If thou be the Son of God, command that these stones be made bread.

4   But he answered and said, It is written, Man shall not live by bread alone, but by every word that proceeds from of the mouth of God.

You must have the mind of Christ which is a **Renewed Mind** in order for the manifestation of the power of God to be present in your life. That also happens in the wilderness.

Remember- The children of Israel, their bodies came out, but their minds were still in bondage, and many of them died in the wilderness. My prayer for the saints of God is:

Don't be the one that does not make it out of the wilderness. It's going to be your mind that he attacks first. To get control of your mind, here are some scriptures that the Lord helped me to get down in my mind which helped me in my time of testing.

1. Loins girt about with truth.

    Truth that which agree with final reality.

John 14:17

[17]Even the Spirit of truth; whom the world cannot receive, because it seeth him not, neither knoweth him: but ye know him; for he dwelleth with you, and shall be in you.

2. Breast plate of righteousness = only the righteous shall see God

II Corinthians 5:21

[21]For he hath made him to be sin for us, who knew no sin; that we might be made the righteousness of God in him.

3. And your feet shod with preparation of the gospel of peace.

Peace also acts as an empire between – soul and spirit.

Roman 5:1

¹Therefore being justified by faith, we have peace with God through our Lord Jesus Christ:

John 14:27

²⁷Peace I leave with you, my peace I give unto you: not as the world giveth, give I unto you. Let not your heart be troubled, neither let it be afraid.

4. Above all, taking the shield of faith, why do you think that this passage is saying above all. If you don't have faith, you won't be able to be properly armed, all the other weapons are tied to faith.

Hebrew 11:6

⁶But without faith it is impossible to please him: for he that cometh to God must believe that he is, and that he is a rewarder of them that diligently seek him.

5. And take the helmet of Salvation-protection for the mind.

Rom 8:6-7

6   For to be carnally minded is death; but to be spiritually minded is life and peace.

7   Because the carnal mind is enmity against God: for it is not subject to the law of God, neither indeed can be. (KJV)

6. And the sword of the spirit which is the word of God.

Hebrew 4:12

For the word of God is quick, and powerful, and sharper than any two-edged sword, piercing even to the dividing asunder of soul and spirit, and of the joints and marrow, and is a discerner of the thoughts and intents of the heart.

7. Praying always with all prayer and supplication in the spirit, and watching there unto with all perseverance and supplication for all saints.

Philippians 4:6

Be careful for nothing; but in every thing by prayer and supplication with thanksgiving let your requests be made known unto God.

8. Garments of praise

Acts 16:25-26

[25]*And at midnight Paul and Silas prayed, and sang praises unto God: and the prisoners heard them.*

[26]*And suddenly there was a great earthquake, so that the foundations of the prison were shaken: and immediately all the doors were opened, and every one's bands were loosed.*

The Lord also showed me when you are going through your wilderness experience don't focus on it. I know that it may seem hard to do, when God shows you trust in him. You will learn it's not as hard as you think it is, when you depend on God for your strength.

The Lord taught me as a child of God I am a servant first. That means I am to serve the people of God no matter what I'm going through. So, that's what I did, I prayed and asked God to show me what I was supposed to be doing with my time. Even as I writing, my trials are not over as far as my eyes can see. But saints of God in my spirit I've already crossed over to the promise land. God has already made me a woman of great faith through my wilderness experience. Please understand just because you are in the wilderness don't give the devil the pleasure by acting like it. Act like you are in the promise land, that's right; give the devil a fit.

God is not going to complicate things, we are the ones who complicate our wilderness experience, because we will not allow God to finish some things in our lives. Remember saints, the work that God is doing in you it's a good work. So sit at the feet of Jesus and let our Heavenly Father work in and work out some things, even as I am writing I am praying that our Father in heaven will teach you to learn to enter into his rest. I also found out when you don't focus on your own trials it shows that you are not a selfish person. You must learn to let God develop you into the great leader that He sees that you are. He feels what you feel.

Hebrews 4:15-16

[15]For we have not an high priest which cannot be touched with the feeling of our infirmities; but was in all points tempted like as we are, yet without sin.

[16]Let us therefore come boldly unto the throne of grace, that we may obtain mercy, and find grace to help in time of need.

Now you see Jesus our precious Lord and Savior, knows what you feel children of God, he was tempted like we are and he over came every snare that the enemy put in his way.

Why?

Because he knew his purpose, you must understand the weapons that Satan uses. There are (3) three areas that he works in:

1. Lust of the eyes – things we see-misguided

2. Lust of the flesh – wrong desire

3. Pride of life – I not God

For we wrestle not against flesh and blood, but against principalities, against powers, against the rulers of the darkness of this world, against spiritual wickedness in high places. The desire of the flesh is what keeps so many saints from the true purpose of God. We must learn to keep Satan under our feet.

PROVISION IN THE WILDERNESS

God will always provide for his children, when he calls you to be tested (Exodus 16:4) bread from heaven, when the children of Israel were in the wilderness He provided manna. (Ex. 16:31)

The children of Israel were required to only get what they needed day by day, with the exception of the Sabbath. When we have a need it is our responsibility to pray to the Heavenly Father for daily provision and also expect God to give you what you need. When God gives you your daily supply be content.

Hebrews 13:5

[5]Let your conversation be without covetousness; and be content with such things as ye have: for he hath said, I will never leave thee, nor forsake thee.

Our Heavenly Father is right in the midst of your test, but sometimes we complain so much about what we used to have. The children of Israel were so angry with God, because they had not imaged what they had to go through to get to the promise land. There hearts were not given to what God wanted to do. I see it this way, they were so used to the old ways of Egypt, it was so hard for them to get used to

God's way of doing things. So time after time they complained, even though they complained God provided for that season. As a result of their unthankful ness they died right in the wilderness. This is why it is so important to understand in all things be content until God is ready to move you from the season that you are in. The Lord's Prayer also teaches that God supplies our daily needs.

Matthew 6:11

[11]Give us this day our daily bread. [12]And forgive us our debts, as we forgive our debtors.

Jesus the one who meets your needs, told us to pray daily, asking him to supply all our needs, we are talking about the time of testing, and that is how you get to know God as your provider. Remember when you're content you are satisfied, do not worry.

Matthew 6:25

[25]Therefore I say unto you, Take no thought for your life, what ye shall eat, or what ye shall drink; nor yet for your body, what ye shall put on. Is not the life more than meat, and the body than raiment?

PRINCIPLES FOR CHAPTER 6

1. The wilderness test will always come before promotion can be granted.

2. You must have the right weapons in the wilderness.

3. Don't focus on the test, focus on Jesus.

4. God always provides in the wilderness.

CHAPTER 7

YOU MUST BE AN HEIR TO OBTAIN GOD'S PROMISE

After these things the word of the LORD came unto Abram in a vision, saying, Fear not, Abram: I am thy shield, and thy exceeding great reward.

And Abram said, LORD God, what wilt thou give me, seeing I go childless, and the steward of my house is this Eliezer of Damascus?

Abram said, behold, to me thou hast given no seed: and, lo, one born in my house is mine heir.

Behold, the word of the LORD came unto him, saying, This shall not be thine heir; but he that shall come forth out of thine own bowels shall be thine heir. And he brought him forth abroad, and said, look now toward heaven, and count the stars, if thou be able to number them: and he said unto him, So shall thy seed be.

And he believed in the LORD; and he counted it to him for righteousness.

Caution!

Now look at what took place as soon as God made a covenant promise about the heir of Abram.

Genesis 16:2

²And Sar'ai said unto Abram, Behold now, the LORD hath restrained me from bearing: I pray thee, go in unto my maid;

it may be that I may obtain children by her. And Abram hearkened to the voice of Sar'ai.

Saints of God I warn you, do not settle for an Ishmael when you can have an Isaac. Ishmael came because of a lack of trust and patience on Sarai behave. No matter what's going on, wait on the Lord to bring your promise to past. Don't try to make it happen yourself. Whenever you have imitations they never bring you peace.

Genesis 21:10

[10]Wherefore she said unto Abraham, Cast out this bondwoman and her son: for the son of this bondwoman shall not be heir with my son, even with Isaac.

Secondly, Duet 13:4 Ye shall walk after the LORD your God, and fear him, and keep his commandments, and obey his voice, and ye shall serve him, and cleave unto him.

You must learn to obey the word of the Lord. Obedience will always bring you the favor of God upon your life.

Numbers 15:39-40

[39]And it shall be unto you for a fringe, that ye may look upon it, and remember all the commandments of the LORD, and do them; and that ye seek not after your own heart and your own eyes, after which ye use to go a whoring:

[40]That ye may remember, and do all my commandments, and be holy unto your God

Also in the beginning of this passage of scripture the Lord gave them tassels to remind them to do the will of God. The tassel's were worn around the hem of there clothes. Just as God gave the children of Israel tassel's to remind them to do the will of God, the reminder God gives us today is the word of God.

Joshua 1:8 (Ponder the word) over and over

⁸This book of the law shall not depart out of thy mouth; but thou shalt meditate therein day and night, that thou mayest observe to do according to all that is written therein: for then thou shalt make thy way prosperous, and then thou shalt have good success.

See saints this passage also teaches us that it's only when you do the word of God you will obtain prosperity and good success. That means your life must show forth fruit, that you are applying the word of God in your everyday living.

Ephesians 1:3-14

³Blessed be the God and Father of our Lord Jesus Christ, who hath blessed us with all spiritual blessings in heavenly places in Christ:

⁴According as he hath chosen us in him before the foundation of the world, that we should be holy and without blame before him in love:

⁵Having predestinated us unto the adoption of children by Jesus Christ to himself, according to the good pleasure of his will,

⁶To the praise of the glory of his grace, wherein he hath made us accepted in the beloved.

⁷In whom we have redemption through his blood, the forgiveness of sins, according to the riches of his grace;

⁸Wherein he hath abounded toward us in all wisdom and prudence;

⁹Having made known unto us the mystery of his will, according to his good pleasure which he hath purposed in himself:

[10]That in the dispensation of the fullness of times he might gather together in one all things in Christ, both which are in heaven, and which are on earth; even in him:

[11]In whom also we have obtained an inheritance, being predestinated according to the purpose of him who worketh all things after the counsel of his own will:

[12]That we should be to the praise of his glory, who first trusted in Christ.

[13]In whom ye also trusted, after that ye heard the word of truth, the gospel of your salvation: in whom also after that ye believed, ye were sealed with that holy Spirit of promise,

[14]Which is the earnest of our inheritance until the redemption of the purchased possession, unto the praise of his glory.

In verse 1:13 you are sealed is seen by some as referring to justification, but that term is used here and emphasis is different. Justification brings acceptance sealing authority, which means you have a right to your inheritance, because of your covenant relationship with God.

PRINCIPLES FOR CHAPTER 7

1. We have to walk in the ways of God before we obtain our covenant blessing.

2. You must wait on God. <u>Sar'ai was impatience</u>, you must be patience.

3. Look for the enemy, whenever God gives you a promise the enemy will try to steal it away from you.

CHAPTER 8

GET READY FOR COVENANT BLESSING

Covenant Defined

A binding and solemn agreement to do or keep from doing a specified thing - *Webster's College Dictionary.*

In other words the bible is full of covenant blessings. God's promise to save men on condition of their believing and confessing and receiving him as their Lord and Savior. Roman's cp. 10-verse 9-10. This is one promise what I am so grateful for salvation. That is where life changing events first take place upon your believing and receiving Christ as your personal Savior.

Covenant blessings are set a side for God's chosen children. In chapter one we talked about hearing and submitting to the voice of the father. Understand when you obey his voice you obey his will.

First Mention

Example #1

Noah received God's first Covenant blessing. Gen 9-9 this promise not to repeat the flood. Gen. 9:15 the rainbow stands eternally as a sign of God's promise. Gen. 9:13

Example #2

To obtain your covenant blessing you must be an heir.

Here in Genesis chapter 15:1-6 we see a conversation taking place between God and Abram concerning the covenant promise of his son.

I don't have to go on and on about what you need to do to obtain your blessing from God. Get before our precious Lord and Saviour and pray for direction. I only gave two examples of people in the word of God. Because that is what he laid upon my heart to do, but we know that there are many.

In concluding, I would like to admonish you my precious brothers and sisters in the Lord to read your bible daily or as often as you can. Seek the face of God for yourself. Because the most important thing that the Lord taught me during my time's of testing was to hide his word in my heart. He always took me back to the word. As I meditated, pondered, repeated his word daily he taught me that He is my provider. But I had to use the principles that God had taught me to use:

(1) You must understand that God is always with you.

(2) Never open a door for fear to get in because when you allow fear to get in you can't have faith in the word of God.

(3) Hold on to the promises of God no matter what you see with your natural eyes. Ask God to give you spiritual insight so you will be able to hold on to his promises.

(4) Gal. 5:17 Never give in to the flesh what your spiritual natures wants. Never give into your corrupt nature being your flesh. Crucify your flesh daily.

(5) Love yourself inspite of your failures. Take your failures as lesson's to teach you what not to do being a man or woman of God.

(6) Fasting and praying must be a part of your life as a child of the king.

(7) Stay on your face before God, acknowledge him before you make major decision.

(8) Worship and praise your father no matter what's going on, that's when you will experience the awesome love of God the most.

(9) Remember worship is where the times of refreshing come.